MINIATURE QUILTS

The Best of

Volume 2

From the Editors of *Miniature Quilts* magazine

D1608922

CHITRA PUBLICATIONS

Chitra Publications
2 Public Avenue
Montrose, Pennsylvania 18801-1220

First Printing: 1999

Library of Congress Cataloging-in-Publication Data

The best of Miniature quilts / [compiled by the editors of miniature
quilts].
     p.   cm.
    ISBN 1-885588-24-0 (v. 2) : $12.95
     1. Quilting--Patterns. 2. Patchwork--Patterns. 3. Appliqué--
Patterns. 4. Miniature quilts.   I. Miniature quilts.
TT835.B363 1994
746.9'7' 0228--dc20   94-3825
                                               CIP

Edited by: The Editors of *Miniature Quilts* magazine
Design and Illustrations: Diane M. Albeck-Grick
Cover Photography: Guy Cali Associates, Inc., Clarks Summit, PA
Inside Photography: Stephen J. Appel Photography, Vestal, NY;
Guy Cali Associates, Inc., Clarks Summit, PA;
Craige's Photography, Montrose, PA;
Van Zandbergen Photography, Brackney, PA

———— *Our Mission Statement* ————
We publish quality quilting magazines
and books that recognize, promote
and inspire self-expression.
We are dedicated to serving
our customers with respect,
kindness and efficiency.

Introduction

Plenty of quilting fun is sure to begin with this collection of 18 best-loved patterns from the pages of *Miniature Quilts* magazine. It's a gold mine for miniature quilt lovers. These minis represent a wide range of styles, sizes and skill levels. The construction methods are varied, too, so you can practice those you're already familiar with or learn something new. In fact, one advantage to making miniatures is that you can try a less familiar technique without a large investment of time and materials. You'll find each pattern is easy to follow and the general stitching guidelines contained in "Mini Stitching Tips" (p. 31) provide a handy reference.

Miniature Quilts magazine has been in publication for over a decade. It began as a special issue of *Quilting Today*, another magazine from Chitra Publications. We soon realized that there was enough interest in making minis to justify a magazine totally devoted to making them. Over the years, that interest has continued to grow at a rapid pace. Construction techniques such as foundation piecing and strip piecing have also evolved, simplifying sewing and making the handling of small pieces easier than ever. You'll get to use many easy construction techniques when making the patterns in this sequel to *The Best of Miniature Quilts, Volume 1*.

Readers of *Miniature Quilts* know how delightful it is to sew minis. Little quilts make thoughtful gifts, add charming accents to home decor and provide hours of creative pleasure. The biggest challenge is in knowing which adorable mini to make first. We think you'll enjoy every page of this long-awaited pattern book!

The Editors of *Miniature Quilts* ♥

Contents

General Directions

Patterns

Mini Stars at Sea

Lose yourself in a sea of scraps!

Jenny Ballway of Evanston, Illinois, found working in scraps quite a challenge while making **"Mini Stars at Sea"** (17" square). Jenny says, "I decided to loosen up a little and chose this pattern so I could use a variety of scraps. It has been a pleasant learning experience. We all have to stretch ourselves sometimes."

QUILT SIZE: 17" square

MATERIALS

Yardage is estimated for 44" fabric.
- Assorted scraps of light and dark blue and black prints
- Fat eighth (11" x 18") yellow
- Fat eighth gold
- Fat eighth yellow print
- 1/4 yard black print
- 1/4 yard light-colored fabric
- 19" square of backing fabric
- 19" square of thin batting
- Paper, muslin or lightweight, non-fusible interfacing for the foundations

CUTTING

Dimensions include a 1/4" seam allowance. Scraps for foundation piecing will be cut as you sew the blocks. Each piece must be at least 1/2" larger on all sides than the section it will cover. Refer to Mini Stitching Tips *as needed.*
- Cut 64: 1" squares, blue scraps
- Cut 4: 5/8" x 14 1/2" strips, yellow, for the first border
- Cut 4: 5/8" x 14 1/2" strips, gold, for the second border
- Cut 4: 1" x 15 1/2" strips, yellow print, for the third border
- Cut 4: 1 1/2" x 17 1/2" strips, black print, for the fourth border
- Cut 2: 1 3/4" x 44" strips, black print, for the binding

DIRECTIONS

Follow the foundation piecing instructions in Mini Stitching Tips *to piece the blocks.*
- Trace the full-size patterns on the foundation material, transferring all lines and numbers and leaving a 1" space between foundations. Cut each one out 1/2" beyond the broken line. Make 16 of Block A, 40 of Block B and 25 of Block C.

For the Four Patch:
- Stitch 1" squares in pairs. Make 32.
- Join pairs to form a Four Patch, as shown. Make 16.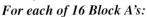

For each of 16 Block A's:
- Use the following fabrics in these positions:
  1 - Four Patch
  2, 3, 4, 5 - light-colored fabric
  6, 7, 8, 9 - blue scraps

For each of 40 Block B's:
- Use the following fabrics in these positions:
  1 - blue scrap
  2, 3, 4, 5 - light-colored fabric

For each of 25 Block C's:
- Use the following fabrics in these positions:
  1 - light-colored fabric
  2, 3, 4, 5 - blue scraps

Full-Size Foundation Patterns for Mini Stars at Sea

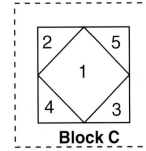

Block C

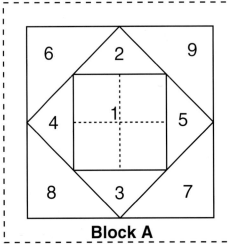

Block A

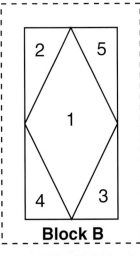

Block B

ASSEMBLY

• Lay out 5 Block C's and 4 Block B's. Join the blocks to form Row 1. Make 5.

C   B   Row 1

• Lay out 5 Block B's and 4 Block A's. Join the blocks to form Row 2. Make 4.

B   A   Row 2

• Lay out the rows, alternating Rows 1 and 2, as shown in the photo. Join the rows to complete the quilt center.

• Measure the length of the quilt. Trim 2 of the 5/8" x 14 1/2" yellow strips to equal that measurement. Stitch them to opposite sides of the quilt.

• Measure the width of the quilt, including the borders. Trim the remaining 5/8" x 14 1/2" yellow strips to equal that measurement. Stitch them to the remaining sides of the quilt.

• In the same manner, trim 2 of the 5/8" x 14 1/2" gold strips to fit the quilt's length and stitch them to opposite sides of the quilt.

• Trim the remaining 5/8" x 14 1/2" gold strips to fit the remaining sides and stitch them to the quilt.

• Trim 2 of the 1" x 15 1/2" yellow print strips to fit the quilt's length and stitch them to opposite sides of the quilt.

• Trim the remaining 1" x 15 1/2" yellow print strips to fit the remaining sides and stitch them to the quilt.

• Trim 2 of the 1 1/2" x 17 1/2" black print strips to fit the quilt's length and stitch them to opposite sides of the quilt.

• Trim the remaining 1 1/2" x 17 1/2" black print strips to fit the remaining sides and stitch them to the quilt.

• If you used paper foundations, remove them now.

• Finish according to *Mini Stitching Tips*, using the 1 3/4" x 44" black print strips for the binding. ❤

Bow Ties and Tuxedos

Stitch your own formal affair!

Rozana Conn of Evergreen, Colorado, "dressed up" "**Bow Ties and Tuxedos**" (19" x 24") with silver lamé borders and three-dimensional bow ties. This clever little quilt was entered in the 1993 Miniatures from the Heart Contest.

QUILT SIZE: 19" x 24"
BLOCK SIZE: 2 1/2" square

MATERIALS

Yardage is estimated for 44" fabric.
• 27 black print scraps, each at least 1 1/2" x 3 1/2"
• 1/4 yard gray print
• 1/8 yard red, for bow ties

• 3" x 6" scrap of white solid
• 3" x 6" scrap of striped fabric
• 1/8 yard silver lamé, for the middle border
• 1/8 yard black print, for the inner border
• 1/2 yard black, for the outer border and binding
• 4" square of glittery plaid, optional

• 21" x 26" piece of backing fabric
• 21" x 26" piece of thin batting

CUTTING

Pattern pieces are full size and include a 1/4" seam allowance, as do all dimensions given.
For each of 27 Bow Tie blocks:
• Cut 2: A, black print

- Cut 1: B, same black print

For the Tuxedo blocks:
- Cut 2: 3" squares, white
- Cut 2: C, stripe fabric
- Cut 2: D, black
- Cut 2: DR, black
- Cut 4: E, red
- Cut 1: 3/4" x 2" strip, red, for the bow tie knots
- Cut 4: 1 3/4" x 3" strips, black

Also:
- Cut 54: A, gray
- Cut 4: 1" x 19" strips, black print, for the inner border
- Cut 4: 1 1/2" x 20" strips, silver lamé, for the middle border
- Cut 4: 2" x 22" strips, black, for the outer border
- Cut 3: 1 3/4" x 40" strips, black, for the binding

DIRECTIONS

For each of the 27 Bow Tie blocks:
- Stitch a black print A to a matching black print B. Start and stop stitching at the 1/4" seamlines.
- Stitch a black print A to the opposite side of the B in the same manner.
- Stitch 2 gray A's to the remaining sides of the B piece. Do not stitch the seams between the A pieces yet.
- Fold the unit in half, right sides together, so that the A pieces line up exactly. Now stitch the seams between the A pieces, starting at the 1/4" seamline at the inside of the block and sewing toward the outside edge.

Backstitch at the beginning of each seam to secure.
- Unfold the block and fold it in the opposite direction. Stitch the other 2 seams to complete a Bow Tie block. Make 27.

For the Tuxedo blocks:
- Stitch a 3" white square between two 1 3/4" x 3" black strips, to make the top half of a Tuxedo block, as shown. Make 2.
- Stitch a D and DR to adjacent sides of a C, as shown, to make the bottom half of a Tuxedo block. Make 2.
- Join the top and bottom halves of the Tuxedo blocks.

ASSEMBLY
- Lay out the Bow Tie blocks and the Tuxedo blocks, referring to the photo, as necessary. Stitch the blocks into rows. Join the rows.
- Measure the length of the quilt. Trim 2 of the 1" x 19" black print strips to equal that measurement. Stitch them to the sides of the quilt.
- Measure the width of the quilt, including the borders. Trim the remaining 1" x 19" black print strips to equal that measurement. Stitch them to the top and bottom of the quilt.
- In the same manner, trim 2 of the

1 1/2" x 20" silver lamé strips to fit the quilt's length and stitch them to the sides of the quilt.
- Trim the remaining 1 1/2" x 20" silver lamé strips to fit the remaining sides and stitch them to the top and bottom of the quilt.
NOTE: Our directions call for solid black outer borders. If you wish, sew a 2" glittery plaid square to each end of the side borders before stitching them to the quilt, as the quiltmaker did.
- Trim 2 of the 2" x 22" black strips to fit the quilt's length and stitch them to the sides of the quilt.
- Trim the remaining 2" x 22" black strips to fit the remaining sides and stitch them to the top and bottom of the quilt.
- To make a bow tie, stitch 2 E's, right sides together, leaving a 1" opening along one long edge for turning. Trim the seam and clip corners. Turn right side out and press. Slipstitch the opening closed. Make 2.
- To make the bow tie knot, fold the 3/4" x 2" red strip in half lengthwise, right sides together. Stitch along its 2" edge. Trim the seam. Turn right side out and press flat. Cut the strip into two 1" pieces. Wrap each piece around the center of a Bow Tie, bringing the raw ends to the back of the tie. Tack the ends together, then tack the bow tie to the top half of each Tuxedo block, as shown in the photo.
- Finish according to *Mini Stitching Tips*, using the 1 3/4" x 40" black strips for the binding. ♥

Full-Size Patterns for Bow Ties and Tuxedos

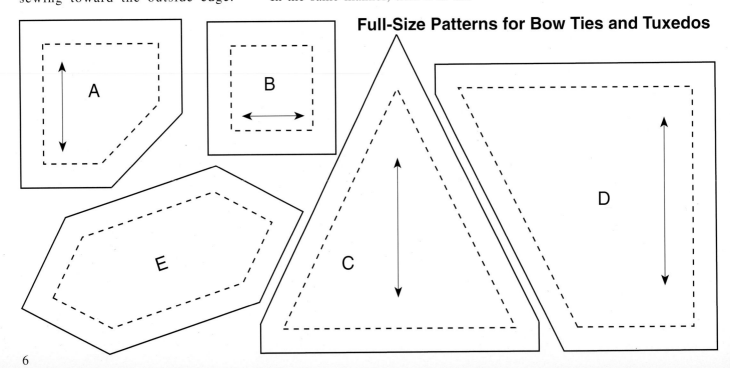

25 Little Anvils

Try our simple techniques to piece this mini in a jiffy!

Each block of **"25 Little Anvils"** (19" square) contains only two fabrics—and none are repeated. Carole Sutton of Lowell, Indiana, used only her leftover fabrics, yet her quilt has a "pulled-together" look.

QUILT SIZE: 19" square
BLOCK SIZE: 3" square

MATERIALS
Yardage is estimated for 44" fabric.
• 25 medium and dark print fabrics each at least 3 3/4" x 6"
• 25 light print fabrics each at least 3 3/4" x 6"
• 3/4 yard blue linear print for the border
• 1/8 yard red print for the binding
• 21" square of backing fabric
• 21" square of thin batting

CUTTING
Dimensions include a 1/4" seam allowance.
For each of 25 Anvil blocks:
NOTE: *Group the pieces for each block as you cut them.*
• Cut 1: 2 3/8" square, medium or dark print
• Cut 1: 1 1/4" x 6" strip, same medium or dark print
• Cut 1: 2 3/8" square, light print
• Cut 1: 1 1/4" x 6" strip, same light print
Also:
• Cut 4: 2 1/4" x 22" strips, blue linear print, centering the design on the strips, for the border
• Cut 2: 1 3/4" x 44" strips, red print, for the binding

DIRECTIONS
For each of 25 Anvil blocks:
• Draw a diagonal line, from corner to corner, on the wrong side of the 2 3/8" light print square. Lay the square on the 2 3/8" medium or dark print square, right sides together, and stitch 1/4" away from both sides of the drawn line, as shown.
• Cut the square on the drawn line to yield 2 pieced squares. Open them and press the seam allowance toward the darker print. Set them aside.
• Stitch the 1 1/4" x 6" medium or dark print strip and the 1 1/4" x 6" light print strip, right sides together, along their length. Press the seam allowance toward the darker strip.
• Cut four 1 1/4" slices from the pieced strip.

• Join 2 slices to make a Four Patch block. Make 2.

• Lay out the pieced squares and Four Patch blocks and join them to make an Anvil block.

• Referring to the photo, lay out the Anvil blocks in 5 rows of 5.
• Stitch the blocks into rows and join the rows.
• Center and stitch a 2 1/4" x 22" blue linear print strip to each side of the quilt. Start and stop stitching 1/4" from the edges and backstitch.
• Miter each corner, referring to *Mini Stitching Tips.*
• Finish according to *Mini Stitching Tips,* using the 1 3/4" x 44" red print strips for the binding. ♥

Crown of Thorns

*A time-tested pattern,
a prizewinning mini!*

Joan Howard of Keene, New Hampshire, had a poster of a quilt from Lancaster County. The full-size version had black prints in alternating blocks but she changed it to this striking red and ecru color combination in her miniature **"Crown of Thorns"** (23" square).

QUILT SIZE: 23" square
BLOCK SIZE: 2 1/2" square

MATERIALS
Yardage is estimated for 44" fabric.
- 2 yards red print
- 2 yards muslin
- 25" square piece of backing fabric
- 25" square of batting

CUTTING
Dimensions include a 1/4" seam allowance.
- Cut 28: 1" x 30" bias strips, red print
- Cut 4: 1" x 27" strips, red print
- Cut 4: 1 3/4" x 28" strips, red print, for the binding
- Cut 28: 1" x 30" bias strips, muslin
- Cut 5: 1" x 27" strips, muslin
- Cut 2: 2 1/4" x 21" strips, muslin
- Cut 2: 2 1/4" x 24" strips, muslin
- Cut 16: 3" squares, muslin
- Cut 4: 5 1/4" squares, muslin; then cut them in quarters diagonally to yield 16 setting triangles
- Cut 2: 3" squares, muslin; then cut them in half diagonally to yield 4 corner triangles

PREPARATION
- Make a plastic template of the pattern piece.
- Mark the diagonal line on the template.

DIRECTIONS
- Stitch a 1" x 30" red print bias strip and a 1" x 30" muslin bias strip, right sides together along their length, to make a pieced strip. Be careful not to stretch the fabrics. Make 28.
- Press the seam allowances toward the red print, then trim them to 1/8".
- Place the template on the strip with the diagonal line on the template directly on the seamline. Trace around the template 20 times. Cut out the squares. You may prefer to use a square ruler and cut twenty 1" pieced squares from each pieced strip. You will need a total of 548 pieced squares.

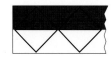

- Join two 1" x 27" red print strips and three 1" x 27" muslin strips, right sides together along their length, in the following order to make a pieced strip: muslin, red print, muslin, red print, muslin. Press the seam allowances toward the red print, then trim them to 1/8".

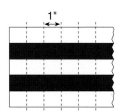

- Cut twenty-five 1" slices from the pieced strip. Label them Row 3.
- Stitch a 1" x 27" red print strip to a 1" x 27" muslin strip, right sides together along their length, to make a pieced strip. Make 2. Press the seam allowances toward the red print, then trim them to 1/8".
- Cut fifty 1" slices from the pieced strips.
- Lay out a block using 16 pieced squares, one Row 3 and 2 red/muslin slices, as shown.

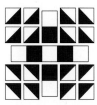

- Stitch the pieced squares into pairs. Join the pairs and slices to complete the rows. Join the rows to complete the block. Trim the seams as necessary.

Make 25 blocks.
• Lay out the blocks on point in 5 rows of 5. Place the 3" muslin squares in the spaces between the blocks. Place the setting triangles around the outside and a corner triangle at each corner.
• Stitch the blocks, squares and triangles into diagonal rows. Join the rows. The triangles will overlap each other when the diagonal rows are sewn.
• Referring to the photo, join 36 pieced squares to make a short pieced border. Make 2.
• In the same manner, join 38 pieced squares to make a long pieced border. Make 2.
• Stitch the short pieced borders to opposite sides of the quilt. Refer to the photo for color placement.
• Stitch the long pieced borders to the remaining sides of the quilt.
• Measure the width of the quilt. Trim the 2 1/4" x 21" muslin strips to equal that measurement. Stitch them to opposite sides of the quilt.
• Measure the quilt, including borders. Trim the 2 1/4" x 24" muslin strips to that measurement. Stitch them to the remaining sides of the quilt.
• Finish according to *Mini Stitching Tips*, using the 1 3/4" x 28" red strips for the binding. ❤

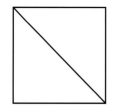

Full-Size Pattern for Crown of Thorns

(Full-Size Quilting Designs for Crown of Thorns are on page 19)

Majestic Mountains

These colorful mountains are right at home in the country or the city!

Julie Berry of Hastings, Nebraska, hand pieced **"Majestic Mountains"** (30 1/4" square) for the 1996 Miniatures from the Heart Contest. Julie says she always does her best and most rewarding work by hand.

QUILT SIZE: 30 1/4" square
BLOCK SIZE: 5" square

MATERIALS
Yardage is estimated for 44" fabric.
• 31 dark green print scraps, each at least 3" x 5"
• 4 dark red print scraps, each at least 3" x 5"
• 15 red and green print scraps, each at least 3" x 5"
• Assorted light print scraps totaling 1/2 yard
• Assorted dark print scraps totaling 3/8 yard
• 1/8 yard red solid
• 1/4 yard tan print, for the inner border
• 3/4 yard green print, for the outer border and binding
• 32 1/2" square of backing fabric
• 32 1/2" square of thin batting

CUTTING
Pattern pieces are full size and include a 1/4" seam allowance, as do all dimensions given.
• Cut 31: A, dark green print
• Cut 4: A, dark red print
• Cut 15: A, red and green print
• Cut 12: A, light print; or cut three 5 1/2" squares, then cut them in quarters diagonally to yield 12 setting triangles
• Cut 2: 3" squares, light print; then

cut them in half diagonally to yield 4 corner triangles
- Cut 16: 1 7/8" squares, light prints. NOTE: *Cut 4 of these squares in half diagonally and set them aside to be used later.*
- Cut 24: 3 3/4" squares, light prints
- Cut 16: 1 7/8" squares, dark prints. NOTE: *Cut 4 of these squares in half diagonally and set them aside to be used later.*
- Cut 24: 3 3/4" squares, dark prints
- Cut 4: 1" x 26" strips, tan print, for the border
- Cut 4: 3/4" x 26" strips, red solid, for the border
- Cut 2: 3 1/2" x 26" strips, green print, for the border
- Cut 2: 3 1/2" x 32" strips, green print, for the border
- Cut 3: 1 3/4" x 44" strips, green print, for the binding

DIRECTIONS

- Stitch 2 print A's together to make a large pieced square, as shown, Make 25. Set them aside.

- Draw a diagonal line from corner to corner on the wrong side of 6 of the 1 7/8" light print squares.
- Place a marked 1 7/8" light print square and an unmarked 1 7/8" light print square right sides together. Stitch 1/4" away from the drawn line on both sides. Make 6.

- Cut the squares apart on the drawn lines to yield 12 light pieced squares. Set them aside.
- Draw a diagonal line on the wrong side of six 1 7/8" dark print squares. Place a marked dark print square and an unmarked 1 7/8" dark print square right sides together. Stitch and cut, as before, to make 12 dark pieced squares. Set them aside.
- Draw diagonal lines from corner to corner on the wrong side of each 3 3/4" light print square. Draw horizontal and vertical lines through the centers.

- Place a marked 3 3/4" light print square and a 3 3/4" dark print square right sides together. Stitch on both sides of the diagonal lines. Make 24.

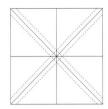

- Cut on the drawn lines to yield 192 small pieced squares.
- Stitch 3 small pieced squares in a row to make Row A, as shown. Make 32.

 Row A

- Stitch 3 small pieced squares in a row to make Row B, as shown. Make 32.

 Row B

- Referring to the Assembly Diagram, lay out the large pieced squares, the light and dark pieced squares and the Row A's and B's in diagonal rows. Note the direction of the seams in the light and dark pieced squares. Place the small light triangles and the small dark triangles where indicated. Place the light print setting and corner triangles around the outside.
- Stitch the units into diagonal rows. Join the rows.
- Measure the width of the quilt. Trim 2 of the 1" x 26" tan print strips to equal that measurement. Stitch them to opposite sides of the quilt.
- Measure the quilt, including the borders. Trim the remaining 1" x 26" tan print strips to equal that measurement. Stitch them to the remaining sides of the quilt.
- Fold the 3/4" x 26" red solid strips in half lengthwise and press.

- Center a pressed strip on one tan border with the long raw edges aligned. Trim off the excess from the ends. Baste it in place inside the seam allowance. Repeat with a pressed strip on the opposite border then on the remaining borders.
- Measure the width of the quilt. Trim the 3 1/2" x 26" green print strips to equal that measurement and stitch them to opposite sides of the quilt.
- Trim the 3 1/2" x 32" green print strips to fit the remaining sides of the quilt. Stitch them to the quilt.
- Finish according to *Mini Stitching Tips*, using the 1 3/4" x 44" green print strips for the binding. ❤

Assembly Diagram

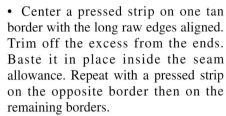

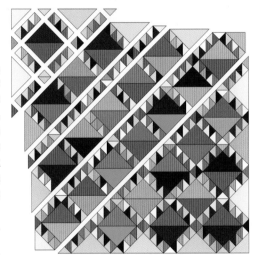

Full-Size Pattern for Majestic Mountains

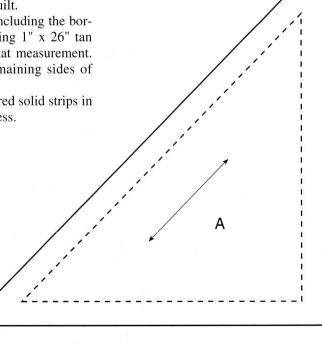

Chellaston

Make little Dresden Plates with a big impact!

Mrs. E. Helen Codd of Poole, Dorset, England, stitched the Dresden Plates in **"Chellaston"** (16 1/4" x 20 1/2") from vintage prints. This little treasure won second prize in the miniature category of a quilt show in England.

QUILT SIZE: 16 1/4" x 20 1/2"
BLOCK SIZE: 3 3/4" square

MATERIALS
Yardage is estimated for 44" fabric.
• Assorted scraps of light and medium prints totaling 1/3 yard
• Yellow print scrap at least 4 1/2" x 6"
• 1/3 yard muslin
• Fat quarter (18" x 22") pink print
• 18 1/2" x 22 1/2" piece of backing fabric
• 18 1/2" x 22 1/2" piece of thin batting

CUTTING
Make templates of each of the pattern pieces and cut them out. Pattern piece A is full size and includes a 1/4" seam allowance. Appliqué pattern piece B is full size and does not include a seam allowance. Trace around template B on the right side of the fabric and add 1/8" to 3/16" turn-under allowance when cutting the pieces out. All other dimensions include a 1/4" seam allowance.
• Cut 144: A, assorted light and medium prints
• Cut 12: B, yellow print
• Cut 2: 1 3/4" x 44" strips, muslin, for the binding
• Cut 12: 4 3/4" squares, muslin
• Cut 2: 1 3/4" x 18" strips, muslin, for the border
• Cut 2: 1 3/4" x 16 1/4" strips, muslin, for the border
• Cut 8: 1" x 4 1/4" strips, pink print, for the sashing

• Cut 5: 1" x 12 3/4" strips, pink print, for the sashing
• Cut 2: 1" x 18" strips, pink print, for the sashing

DIRECTIONS
For each of 12 blocks:
• Place 2 print A's right sides together. Stitch, starting at the curved edge and stopping 1/4" from the outside edge, backstitching to secure. Make 6.

• Join the 6 pairs of A's to make a ring, stopping 1/4" from the outside edges and backstitching to secure.

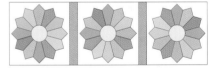

• Press the outside edge of the ring under 1/4". Center and pin the ring on a 4 3/4" muslin square. Appliqué the outside edge of the ring to the muslin square.
• Pin a yellow print B to the center of the ring. Use the tip of your needle to turn under the allowance as you appliqué the B in place to complete a Dresden Plate block.
• Press the block from the wrong side. Trim it to 4 1/4" square, keeping the plate centered.
• Lay out 3 Dresden Plate blocks

and two 1" x 4 1/4" pink print sashing strips. Join them to make a row. Make 4.

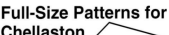

• Stitch a 1" x 12 3/4" pink print strip between each row and one on each end. Stitch 1" x 18" pink print strips to the long sides.
• Stitch 1 3/4" x 18" muslin strips to the long sides of the quilt.
• Stitch 1 3/4" x 16 1/4" muslin strips to the remaining sides of the quilt.
• Finish according to *Mini Stitching Tips*, using the 1 3/4" x 44" muslin strips for the binding. ♥

Full-Size Patterns for Chellaston

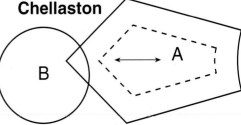

Happy New Year

Precision piecing you can be proud of!

Like an explosion of fireworks in the night sky, Linnea Hassing Nielsen's **"Happy New Year"** (19" square) displays radiant stars against a dark background. Linnea's quilt won 1st place in the Strip Pieced category in the 1996 Miniatures from the Heart Contest.

QUILT SIZE: 19" square

MATERIALS
Yardage is estimated for 44" fabric.
- Fat eighth (11" x 18") red and black print (color 1)
- Fat eighth pink print (color 2)
- Fat eighth multi-colored print with black background (color 3)
- Fat eighth tan print (color 4)
- Fat eighth yellow print (color 5)
- 2/3 yard black
- 21" square piece of backing fabric
- 21" square piece of thin batting

CUTTING
Dimensions include a 1/4" seam allowance.
NOTE: *Make a chart for easy reference by taping a small piece of each fabric to an index card and numbering them.*
For the quilt center:
- Cut 4: 7/8" x 14" strips, color 1
- Cut 10: 7/8" x 18" strips, color 1
- Cut 2: 7/8" x 14" strips, color 2
- Cut 6: 7/8" x 18" strips, color 2
- Cut 4: 7/8" x 14" strips, color 3
- Cut 6: 7/8" x 18" strips, color 3
- Cut 4: 7/8" x 14" strips, color 4
- Cut 6: 7/8" x 18" strips, color 4
- Cut 2: 7/8" x 14" strips, color 5
- Cut 4: 7/8" x 18" strips, color 5
- Cut 8: 2 5/8" squares, black
- Cut 2: 4 5/16" squares, black; then

cut them in quarters diagonally to yield 8 setting triangles
- Cut 4: A, black
- Cut 4: AR, black
Also:
- Cut 2: 3/4" x 15 1/8" strips, color 3, for the narrow border
- Cut 2: 3/4" x 15 5/8" strips, color 3, for the narrow border
- Cut 2: 1 3/4" x 44" strips, black, for the binding
For the star border:
- Cut 64: 7/8" squares each of colors 1, 2, 4 and 5
- Cut 8: 1 1/4" squares each of colors 1, 2, 4 and 5
- Cut 128: 7/8" squares, black
- Cut 128: 7/8" x 1 1/4" strips, black
- Cut 32: 1 1/16" x 2" strips, black

DIRECTIONS
For the quilt center:
- The following diagram represents one of the 8 pieced diamonds that form the Center Star. The numbers refer to the 5 fabrics used. Note that each row is pieced from 3 or 4 of the 5 fabrics and fabric positions vary in order to develop the pattern.

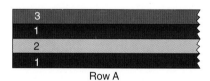

Center Star Diamond

- Begin by strip piecing units for Row A. Gather the 7/8" x 14" strips you need for Row A, arranging them according to the Center Star diamond diagram (1, 2, 1, 3). Stitch the strips together in rows, as shown. Trim the seams to 1/8". Label the unit "Row A" and set it aside.

Row A

- In the same way, stitch together the strips for Row B (2, 1, 3, 4). Label the unit "Row B".
- Stitch the strips for Rows C (1, 3, 4, 5) and D (3, 4, 5, 4) in the same manner. Label the units.
- Take the unit you made for Row A. Mark a line on the 45° angle starting at the lower left edge, as shown. Trim off the corner of the unit on the marked line.

- Measure 7/8" from the trimmed edge. Mark the 45° angle again and cut. With each cut you are making a pieced strip of diamonds. Make 8 of these strips. Stack them and label the stack "Row A". Set it aside.

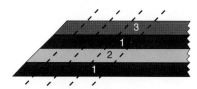

• Follow the same procedure with the remaining 3 pieced units (Rows B, C and D), cutting 8 strips from each unit. Stack the strips and label the stacks B, C and D. Set them aside.

• Lay out one strip from each stack. Be sure the color placement matches the Center Star diamond diagram. Pin the strips together, carefully matching the diamonds at the 1/4" seamline. Join the rows to complete the first Center Star diamond. Make 8.

• Following the same procedure, join 7/8" x 18" strips to make units E, F, G and H for the pieced diamonds that form the Broken Star. Note the color placement in each row when preparing the units. Make 2 of each unit.

Row E	Row F	Row G	Row H
1	2	5	4
3	1	2	5
4	3	1	2
1	4	3	1

Broken Star Diamond

• Cut 12 strips from each unit. Stack and label them Rows E through H, making 2 stacks for each row. Set them aside.

• Lay out one strip from each row, referring to the Broken Star diamond diagram for color placement. Pin and stitch as before. Make 24 Broken Star diamonds.

ASSEMBLY

• Lay out 2 Center Star pieced diamonds and stitch them together. NOTE: *Stop stitching 1/4" from the outer edge and backstitch.* Make 4. In the same manner, join the 4 pairs to complete the Center Star, as shown.

• Lay out the eight 2 5/8" black squares in the spaces between the dia-

mond-shaped units, as shown.

• Set in the black squares to complete the Center Star section.

• Referring to the photo for color placement, stitch the Broken Star pieced diamond units together in 3's, as shown. Stop stitching 1/4" from the outer edges and backstitch, as before. Make 8 three-diamond units.

• Lay out the 8 three-diamond units and the Center Star section, as shown.

• Set in the 3-diamond units. Start and stop stitching 1/4" from the edges, backstitching at each end. NOTE: *Do not stitch the seams connecting the 3-diamond units to each other yet.*

• Lay out the assembled unit, 4 black A's, 4 black AR's and 8 black setting triangles, as shown.

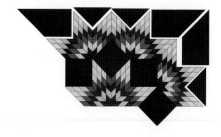

• Set in the 8 black setting triangles.

• Set in a black A and a black AR in each corner.

• Miter the corners, joining the pieced diamonds and the black A's in one continuous seam.

• Stitch the seams between the remaining 3-diamond units; stop at the intersection where the diamonds and the black square meet and backstitch to secure the seam.

• Stitch the 3/4" x 15 1/8" color 3 strips to opposite sides of the quilt.

• Stitch the 3/4" x 15 5/8" color 3 strips to the remaining sides of the quilt.

For the star border:

• Draw diagonal lines on the wrong sides of eight of the 7/8" color 1 squares.

• Position a marked square on a 7/8" x 1 1/4" black strip, right sides together, as shown.

• Stitch on the drawn line. Press the colored square toward the corner and trim the seam allowance. Repeat at the other end of the strip with another 7/8" color 1 square to complete a pieced unit, as shown. Make 4.

• Assemble a border star using four 7/8" black squares, 4 pieced units and a 1 1/4" color 1 square, as shown. Make 8.

• In the same manner, make 8 border stars each using colors 2, 4, and 5.

• Lay out 7 border stars between eight 1 1/16" x 2" black strips, referring to the photograph for color placement. Stitch them together, as shown, to form a short star border. Make 2.

• Lay out eight 1 1/16" x 2" black strips between 9 border stars, again checking for color placement. Stitch them together to form a long star (continued on the bottom of page 15)

Blizzard of '96

These cozy little cottages warm the long winter days.

Mary Ellen Sparks of Philippi, West Virginia, made **"Blizzard of '96"** (12 1/2" square) to remind her of the prettiest days of winter. Mary Ellen enjoys the white snow swirling against the blue sky and dark evergreen trees. With record snowfalls that winter, she has plenty of pretty days to remember!

QUILT SIZE: 12 1/2" square
BLOCK SIZE: 3" square

MATERIALS
Yardage is estimated for 44" fabric.
• Fat quarter (18" x 22") white-on-white print
• Scrap of white-on-white check at least 3" x 6"
• Fat eighth (11" x 18") green pin-dot
• Fat eighth blue print for sky
• Scrap of blue pin-dot at least 4" square
• Scrap of blue print at least 4" x 5"
• Scrap of gold
• Scrap of brown print
• 14 1/2" square of backing fabric

• 14 1/2" square of thin batting
• Paper, muslin or lightweight, non-fusible interfacing for the foundations

CUTTING
Dimensions include a 1/4" seam allowance. Fabric for foundation piecing will be cut as you sew the blocks. Each piece must be at least 1/2" larger on all sides than the section it will cover. Refer to Mini Stitching Tips *as needed.*
• Cut 4: 2" x 14 1/2" strips, white-on-white print, for the border
• Cut 2: 1 3/4" x 30" strips, white-on-white print, for the binding

DIRECTIONS
Follow the foundation piecing instructions in Mini Stitching Tips *to piece the blocks.*
• Trace the full-size patterns on the foundation material transferring all lines and numbers and leaving a 1" space between foundations. Make 4 of the corner Pineapple pattern, one of the center Pineapple pattern, and 4 of each house section. Cut each one out 1/2" beyond the broken line.
For each of 4 corner Pineapple blocks:
• Use the following fabrics in these positions:

Full-Size Foundation Patterns for Blizzard of '96

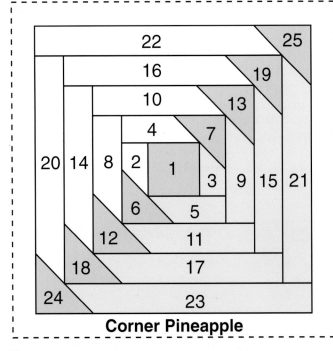

Corner Pineapple

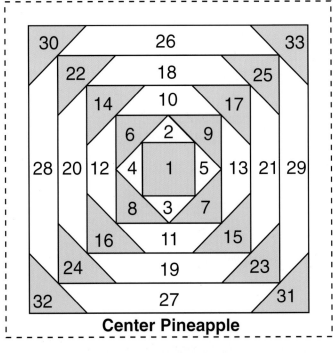

Center Pineapple

1 - green pin-dot
2 - white-on-white print
3 - blue sky print
4 - white-on-white print
5 - blue sky print
6, 7 - green pin-dot
8 - white-on-white print
9 - blue sky print
10 - white-on-white print
11 - blue sky print
12, 13 - green pin-dot
14 - white-on-white print
15 - blue sky print
16 - white-on-white print
17 - blue sky print
18, 19 - green pin-dot
20 - white-on-white print
21 - blue sky print
22 - white-on-white print
23 - blue sky print
24, 25 - green pin-dot

For the center Pineapple block:
• Use the following fabrics in these positions:
    1 - green pin-dot
    2, 3, 4, 5 - white-on-white print
    6, 7, 8, 9 - green pin-dot
    10, 11, 12, 13 - white-on-white print
    14, 15, 16, 17 - green pin-dot
    18, 19, 20, 21 - white-on-white print
    22, 23, 24, 25 - green pin-dot
    26, 27, 28, 29 - white-on-white print
    30, 31, 32, 33 - green pin-dot

For the chimney sections:
• Use the following fabrics in these positions:
    1 - brown
    2, 3, 4 - blue sky fabric

For the roof sections:
• Use the following fabrics in these positions:
    1 - white-on-white check

2 - blue print
3, 4 - blue sky fabric

For the house sections:
• Use the following fabrics in these positions:
    1 - gold
    2, 3, 4 - blue pin-dot
    5 - blue print
    6 - green pin-dot
    7 - blue print
    8 - white-on-white print
• Baste each foundation in the seam allowance, halfway between the stitching line and the broken line, to hold the fabrics in place.
• Trim each foundation on the broken line.
• Join a chimney, a roof and a house

section to complete a house block. Make 4.
• Lay out the blocks in 3 rows of 3, referring to the photo for placement. Stitch the blocks into rows and join the rows.
• Center and stitch a 2" x 14 1/2" white-on-white strip to each side of the quilt. Start and stop stitching 1/4" from the edges and backstitch.
• If you used paper foundations, remove them now.
• Miter each corner, referring to *Mini Stitching Tips*.
• Finish according to *Mini Stitching Tips*, using the 1 3/4" x 30" white-on-white print strips for the binding. ♥

Full-Size Foundation Patterns for Blizzard of '96

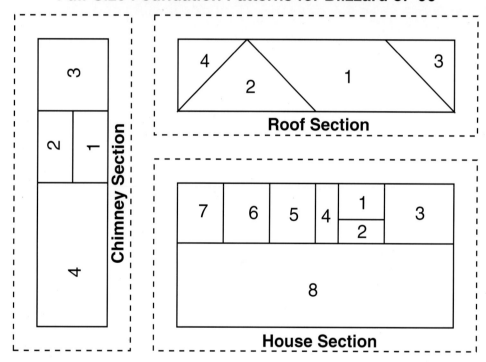

Chimney Section

Roof Section

House Section

Happy New Year
(continued from page 13)

border. Make 2.
• Stitch the short star borders to opposite sides of the quilt.
• Stitch the long star borders to the remaining sides of the quilt.
• Finish according to *Mini Stitching Tips*, using the 1 3/4" x 44" black strips for the binding. ♥

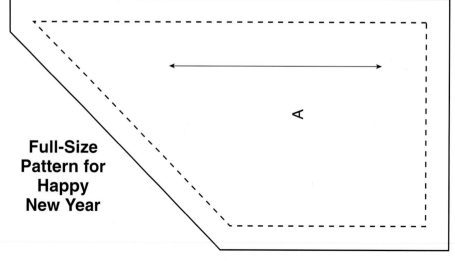

Full-Size Pattern for Happy New Year

A

Gingerbread Play

A wonderful, whimsical mini!

Lisa Caryl of Colo, Iowa, designed **"Gingerbread Play"** (18 1/2" x 21 1/2"), getting her inspiration from plaids she had just purchased. Lisa hand appliquéd, machine pieced and hand quilted her mini, and embellished it with old and new buttons.

QUILT SIZE: 18 1/2" x 21 1/2"
BLOCK SIZE: 3" x 4"

MATERIALS
Yardage is estimated for 44" fabric.
• Assorted red and green plaid fabrics for the gingerbread people and the borders
• 1/4 yard muslin for the backgrounds and the inner border
• 1/8 yard gingerbread fabric
• 1/8 yard red plaid for the outer border
• 1/8 yard plaid for the binding
• 20 1/2" x 23 1/2" piece of backing fabric
• 20 1/2" x 23 1/2" piece of thin batting
• 1/2" buttons for embellishment
• 3 /16" buttons for the gingerbread people
• Clear template plastic
• Permanent fine-point pens for marking the faces

PREPARATION
• Trace the full-size head, hand, foot, dress, overall, and shirt patterns on the template plastic. Cut them out.

CUTTING
Appliqué pieces are full size and do not include a seam allowance. Trace around the templates on the right side of the fabric and add 1/8" to 3/16" turn-under allowance when cutting the pieces out. All other dimensions include a 1/4" seam allowance.
• Cut 9: heads, gingerbread fabric
• Cut 18: hands, gingerbread fabric
• Cut 18: feet, gingerbread fabric
• Cut 5: dresses, assorted plaids
• Cut 4: overalls, assorted plaids
• Cut 4: shirts, assorted plaids
• Cut 90: 1 1/2" squares, assorted plaids
• Cut 8: 1 1/2" x 5 1/2" strips, assorted plaids
• Cut 9: 3 1/2" x 4 1/2" rectangles, muslin, for the background
• Cut 2: 1" x 18 1/2" strips, muslin, for the inner border
• Cut 2: 1" x 16 1/2" strips, muslin, for the inner border
• Cut 4: 2" x 19 1/2" strips, red plaid, for the outer border
• Cut 2: 1 3/4" x 44" strips, plaid, for the binding

DIRECTIONS
• Using a light box or a brightly lit window, place each 3 1/2" x 4 1/2" muslin rectangle over the full-size pattern. Center and lightly trace the design on each rectangle. Trace 5 gingerbread girls and 4 gingerbread boys.

• Use the tip of your needle to turn under the seam allowance as you appliqué each piece in place. Use the drawn line for placement. There is no need to turn under the allowance where pieces overlap. For each block, appliqué the head, hands, and feet in place.
• For the gingerbread boys, appliqué the shirt in place. Then appliqué the overalls. Press the blocks lightly from the back. Stitch a 3/16" button at each shoulder.
• For the gingerbread girls, appliqué the dress in place. Press the blocks lightly from the back. Stitch two 3/16" buttons at the neck edge of the dress.
• Mark faces on the gingerbread people with a permanent fine-point marker.
• Lay out the 9 gingerbread people blocks, the ninety 1 1/2" squares, and the eight 1 1/2" x 5 1/2" strips as shown in the Assembly Diagram on page 27. Rearrange the blocks, squares and strips until the arrangement pleases you.
• Stitch them into rows. Join the rows.
• Measure the length of the quilt. Trim the 1" x 18 1/2" muslin strips to equal that measurement. Stitch them to the sides of the quilt.
• Measure the width of the quilt,

(continued on page 27)

Don't Tread on My Heart

Plaids and checks and stripes, Oh My!

Plaids, stripes and earthy colors give **"Don't Tread on My Heart"** (20 1/2" x 29 1/2") a country look. Ann Bade of Nebraska City, Nebraska, miniaturized this charmer from a Star Quilt Company pattern. (See ordering information on page 19.)

QUILT SIZE: 20 1/2" x 29 1/2"
BLOCK SIZE: 3 1/4" x 4 3/4"

MATERIALS
Yardage is estimated for 44" fabric.
• Assorted scraps of plaids, prints, checks and stripes
• 1/4 yard small-scale black plaid, for the border
• 1/4 yard large-scale black plaid, for the binding
• 22 1/2" x 31 1/2" piece of backing fabric
• 22 1/2" x 31 1/2" piece of thin batting

CUTTING
Pattern pieces are full size and include a 1/4" seam allowance, as do all dimensions given.
For each of 16 blocks:
NOTE: *Group the pieces for each block as you cut them.*
• Cut 1: B, G, H, J, K and M, first fabric, for the star

• Cut 1: A, D, L, N and P, second fabric, for the heart
• Cut 1: C, E, F, Q and R, third fabric, for the background
Also:
NOTE: *Stack and label strips one through 8 as you cut them.*
• Cut 2: 1 1/4" x 10 1/4" strips, assorted fabrics - Strip 1
• Cut 4: 1 1/4" x 7" strips, assorted fabrics - Strip 2
• Cut 2: 1 1/4" x 3 3/4" strips, assorted fabrics - Strip 3
• Cut 8: 1 1/4" x 6" strips, assorted fabrics - Strip 4
• Cut 2: 1 1/4" x 11" strips, assorted fabrics - Strip 5
• Cut 4: 1 1/4" x 7 3/4" strips, assorted fabrics - Strip 6
• Cut 2: 1 1/4" x 4 1/2" strips, assorted fabrics - Strip 7
• Cut 8: 1 1/4" x 6 3/4" strips, assorted fabrics - Strip 8
• Cut additional 1 1/4"-wide strips of

assorted fabrics in various lengths, from 4" to 12", to total 95".
NOTE: *You will join these strips, end to end, to make 2 pieced strips 17 1/2" long and 2 pieced strips 28" long.*
• Cut 2: 1 3/4" x 19" strips, small-scale black plaid, for the border
• Cut 2: 1 3/4" x 31" strips, small-scale black plaid, for the border
• Cut 3: 1 3/4" x 44" strips, large-scale black plaid, for the binding

DIRECTIONS
For each block:
• Stitch B and C to A to make Unit 1, as shown.

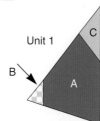

Unit 1

17

- Stitch E and F to D to make Unit 2, as shown.

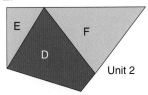

- Stitch H and J to G to make Unit 3, as shown.

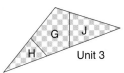

- Stitch K and L together to make Unit 4, as shown.

- Stitch N and P to M to make Unit 5, as shown.

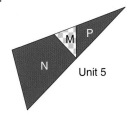

- Lay out Units 1 through 5, as shown.

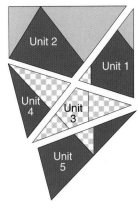

- Join Units 1 and 2 to form the top of the heart.
- Join Units 3, 4 and 5 to form the bottom of the heart.
- Join the top and bottom of the heart.
- Stitch Q to the left side of the heart. Stitch R to the right side of the heart to complete the block, as shown. Make 16.

- Lay out 4 rows of 4 blocks, grouping the blocks in units as shown in the photo and Assembly Diagram.
- Join the blocks to form units within the rows. Row 1 consists of a triple block unit and a single block. Rows 2 and 4 consist of 2 double block units. Row 3 consists of a single block and a triple block unit.
- Lay out all of the strips one through 8 and the block units according to the Assembly Diagram.
- Stitch the strips to the single blocks and the block units in the following order: top, left side, bottom, right side.
- Stitch the units into rows and join the rows.
- Stitch enough of the 1 1/4"-wide strips together, end to end, to make a pieced strip that measures 1 1/4" x 17 1/2". Make 2.
- Stitch enough of the 1 1/4"-wide strips together, end to end, to make a pieced strip that measures 1 1/4" x 28". Make 2.

- Measure the width of the quilt. Trim the 1 1/4" x 17 1/2" pieced strips to equal that measurement. Stitch them to the top and bottom of the quilt.
- Measure the length of the quilt, including the borders. Trim the 1 1/4" x 28" pieced strips to equal that measurement. Stitch them to the remaining sides of the quilt.
- In the same manner, trim the 1 3/4" x 19" small-scale black plaid strips to fit the quilt's width and stitch them to the top and bottom of the quilt.
- Trim the 1 3/4" x 31" small-scale black plaid strips to fit the remaining sides and stitch them to the quilt.
- Finish according to *Mini Stitching Tips*, using the 1 3/4" x 44" large-scale black plaid strips for the binding. ❤

Assembly Diagram

Full-Size Patterns for Don't Tread on My Heart

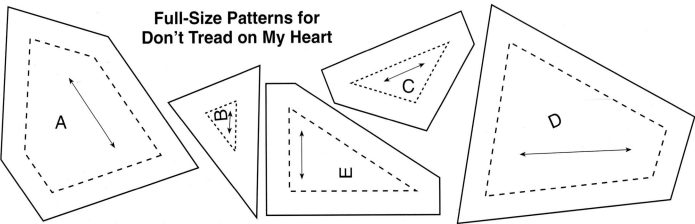

Full-Size Patterns for Don't Tread on My Heart

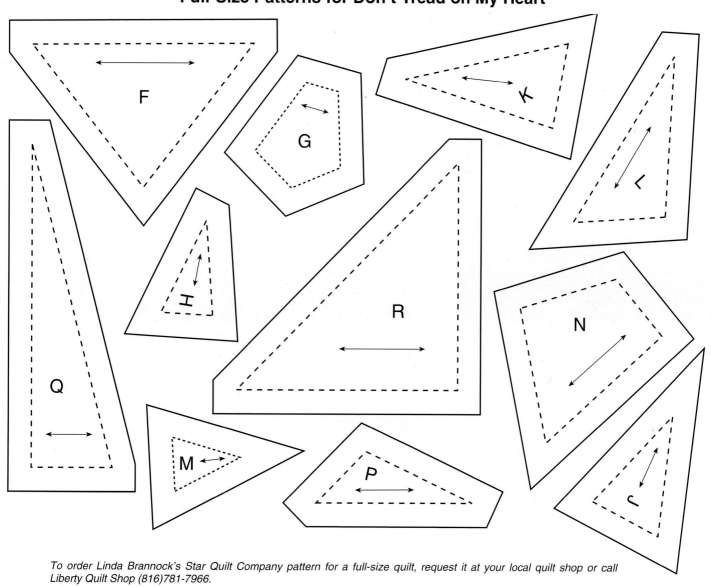

To order Linda Brannock's Star Quilt Company pattern for a full-size quilt, request it at your local quilt shop or call Liberty Quilt Shop (816)781-7966.

Full-Size Quilting Designs for Crown of Thorns

(Pattern begins on page 8)

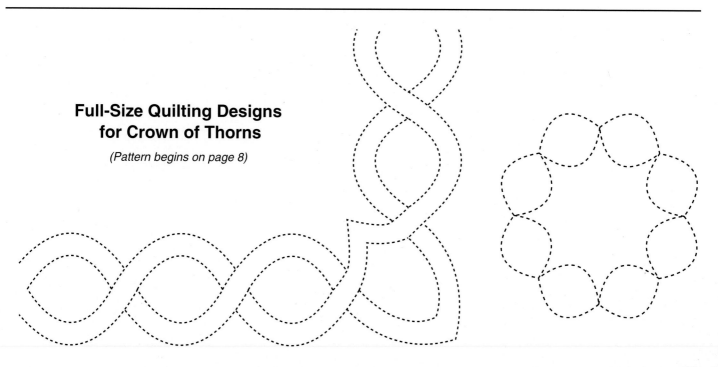

Indiana Stars

Careful color placement is the key to this dynamic quilt!

This Indiana Puzzle design only looks challenging! Careful placement of colors allows the interlocking design to emerge. Shanna Smith Suttner of Chesterfield, Missouri, made **"Indiana Stars"** (8 3/4" x 10 1/4") for the 1994 Miniatures from the Heart Contest.

QUILT SIZE: 8 3/4" x 10 1/4"
BLOCK SIZE: 3/4" square

MATERIALS
Yardage is estimated for 44" fabric.
- 6" squares of 12 different bright fabrics
- 1/4 yard black
- 1/8 yard white
- 10 3/4" x 12 1/4" piece of backing fabric
- 10 3/4" x 12 1/4" piece of thin batting

CUTTING
Pattern piece A is full size and includes a 1/4" seam allowance, as do all dimensions given.
From each of the twelve 6" squares:
- Cut 6: A, or cut three 1 5/8" squares, then cut each in half diagonally
- Cut 1: 1 1/4" square
- Cut 7: 7/8" squares
Also:
- Cut 1: 7/8" x 44" strip, white
- Cut 1: 7/8" x 44" strip, black
- Cut 4: 7/8" x 8" strips, black, for the inner border
- Cut 4: 1 1/4" x 10" strips, black, for the outer border
- Cut 1: 1 3/4" x 44" strip, black, for the binding

DIRECTIONS
- Stitch the 7/8" x 44" white strip to the 7/8" x 44" black strip, right sides together along their length, to form a pieced strip. Press the seam allowance toward the black strip, then trim it to 1/8".
- Cut forty-eight 7/8" slices from the pieced strip.

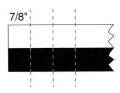

- Join the slices in pairs, alternating the black and white squares to form a Four Patch. Make 24.
- Lay out 20 Four Patch blocks and twelve 1 1/4" squares, as shown in the Assembly Diagram. Then place matching A's next to each 1 1/4" square. Complete the layout by placing 14 of the remaining 24 A's randomly around the outside edge. You will have 10 A's left to use in another project.
- Join pairs of A's to form pieced squares, then return them to the layout.
- Stitch the squares into rows. Join the rows.
- Measure the length of the quilt. Trim 2 of the 7/8" x 8" black strips to equal that measurement. Stitch them to the long sides of the quilt.
- Measure the width of the quilt, including the borders. Trim the remaining 7/8" x 8" black strips to equal that measurement. Stitch them to the remaining sides of the quilt.
- Make 2 pieced rows, each consisting of sixteen 7/8" squares.

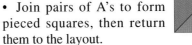

- Stitch the pieced rows to the short sides of the quilt.
- Make 2 pieced rows each consisting of twenty-two 7/8" squares. You will have 8 squares left to use in another project.
- Stitch the pieced rows to the remaining sides of the quilt.
- Trim 2 of the 1 1/4" x 10" black strips to fit the short sides of the quilt.
- Stitch a Four Patch to each end of these black strips to form pieced strips, as shown. Set them aside.

- Trim the remaining 1 1/4" x 10" black strips to fit the long sides of the quilt. Stitch them to the quilt.
- Stitch the pieced strips to the remaining sides of the quilt.
- Finish according to *Mini Stitching Tips*, using the 1 3/4" x 44" black strips for the binding. ❤

(Full-Size Pattern is on page 23)

Assembly Diagram

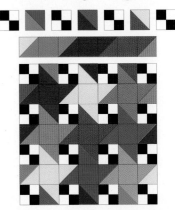

Great-Grandmother's Scraps

Preserve the tiniest of scraps in these blocks.

The scrap fabrics that compose **"Great-Grandmother's Scraps"** (20 1/8" square) have been passed down among four generations—from Anne M. Huskey-Lockard's great-grandmother, to her grandmother, to her mother and eventually to Anne. The quiltmaker from Peru, Indiana, has created a wonderful way to preserve her ties to her ancestors.

QUILT SIZE: 20 1/8" square
BLOCK SIZE: 1 5/8" square

MATERIALS
Yardage is estimated for 44" fabric.
- Assorted print scraps
- 1/3 yard white
- 1/8 yard brown print for the binding
- 22 1/4" square of backing fabric
- 22 1/4" square of thin batting

CUTTING
Pattern pieces are full size and include a 1/4" seam allowance, as do all dimensions given.
For each of 49 blocks:
- Cut 4: A, same print; or cut one 2 1/2" square, then cut it in quarters diagonally to yield 4 triangles
- Cut 4: B, white
- Cut 1: C, matching print
Also:
- Cut 36: 2 1/8" squares, white
- Cut 6: 3 5/8" squares, white; then cut them in quarters diagonally to yield 24 setting triangles
- Cut 2: 2 1/8" squares, white; then cut them in half diagonally to yield 4 corner triangles
- Cut 2: 2" x 17 1/2" strips, white, for the border
- Cut 2: 2" x 20 1/2" strips, white, for the border
- Cut 2: 1 3/4" x 44" strips, brown print, for the binding

DIRECTIONS
- Stitch a white B between matching print A's, as shown, to form a pieced triangle. Make 2.

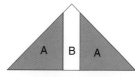

- Stitch a matching print C between white B's to form a pieced strip, as shown.

- Stitch the pieced strip between the pieced triangles to complete a block. Make 49.

- Lay out the 49 blocks and the thirty-six 2 1/8" white squares in diagonal rows. Place setting and corner triangles around the outside. Refer to the Assembly Diagram as needed.
- Stitch the blocks, squares and triangles in diagonal rows. Join the rows.
- Measure the length of the quilt. Trim the 2" x 17 1/2" white strips to equal that measurement. Stitch them to opposite sides of the quilt.
- Measure the width of the quilt, including the borders. Trim the 2" x 20 1/2" white strips to equal that measurement. Stitch them to the remaining sides of the quilt.
- Finish according to *Mini Stitching Tips*, using the 1 3/4" x 44" brown print strips for the binding. ♥

(Full-Size Patterns are on page 23)

Assembly Diagram

Tree of Life

Branch out and piece this classic!

Ann Bade of Nebraska City, Nebraska, gave many scraps new vitality in **"Tree of Life"** (11" x 14 1/2"). Her quilt reflects the touch of yesteryear present in the many antique quilts she admires.

QUILT SIZE: 11" x 14 1/2"
BLOCK SIZE: 2 1/2" square

MATERIALS
Yardage is estimated for 44" fabric.
• 60 assorted medium to dark print scraps at least 1 3/8" square
• 48 assorted light print scraps at least 1 3/8" square
• Fat eighth (11" x 18") red print
• Fat eighth second red print
• Fat eighth tan print
• 1/8 yard navy blue plaid
• 13" x 16 1/2" piece of backing fabric
• 13" x 16 1/2" piece of thin batting

CUTTING
Pattern pieces are full size and include a 1/4" seam allowance, as do all dimensions given.
• Cut 6: 3" squares red print
• Cut 2: 2 3/4" squares, red print, then cut them in half diagonally to yield 4 corner triangles
• Cut 3: 4 7/8" squares, red print, then cut them in quarters diagonally to yield 12 setting triangles. You will use 10.
• Cut 48: 1 3/8" squares, medium or dark prints
• Cut 48: 1 3/8" squares, light prints
• Cut 24: C, medium or dark prints; or cut twelve 1 3/8" squares, then cut them in half diagonally to yield 24 triangles
• Cut 12: A, tan print

• Cut 12: AR, tan print
• Cut 12: C, tan print
• Cut 12: 1" squares, tan print
• Cut 24: D, tan print; or cut twelve 1 7/8" squares, then cut them in half diagonally to yield 24 triangles
• Cut 12: 1" squares, second red print
• Cut 12: B, second red print
• Cut 36: C, second red print; or cut eighteen 1 3/8" squares, then cut them in half diagonally to yield 36 triangles
• Cut 2: 1 3/4" x 44" strips, navy blue plaid, for the binding

DIRECTIONS
• Draw a diagonal line from corner to corner on the wrong side of each 1 3/8" light print square, as shown.

• Place a marked square on a 1 3/8" medium or dark print square, right sides together. Sew 1/4" from each side of the drawn line, as shown. Make 48.

• Cut on the drawn line. Open the squares and press the seams toward the dark triangles. You will have 96 pieced squares. Trim the "dog ears."

• Lay out one medium or dark print C, 2 pieced squares and one 1" second red print square. Stitch them together to make pieced strip A, as shown. Make 12.

Strip A

• Lay out one second red print C, 3 pieced squares and one 1" tan print square. Stitch them together to make pieced strip B, as shown. Make 12.

Strip B

• Stitch a pieced strip A and a pieced strip B together, as shown.

• Stitch a tan print D to the end to complete Unit 1, as shown. Make 12.

Unit 1

• Lay out one medium or dark print C and one pieced square. Stitch them together to make pieced strip C as shown. Make 12.

Strip C

- Lay out one second red print C and 2 pieced squares. Stitch them together to make pieced strip D, as shown. Make 12.

Strip D

- Stitch a pieced strip C and a pieced strip D together, as shown.

- Stitch a tan print D to the end to complete Unit 2, as shown. Make 12.

D

Unit 2

- Set in a tan print A on the left side of a second red print B, as shown. Stitch from the edge to the marked corner and backstitch at the marked dot to secure the seam. Clip the B piece from the edge to the mark without clipping any stitches.

A

B·

- Pivot the B piece and align the raw edges. Stitch from the edge to the marked corner and backstitch at the marked dot.
- Set in a tan print AR on the opposite side of the B.
- Stitch a tan print C to the bottom of the trunk unit, as shown.
- Stitch a second red print C to the top of the trunk unit, as shown, to complete Unit 3. Make 12.

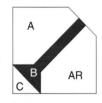

A

B

C

AR

C

Unit 3

- Stitch a Unit 2 to a Unit 3 to make a partial block, as shown.

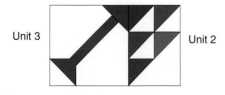

Unit 3

Unit 2

- Stitch a Unit 1 to the partial block to complete the Tree block, as shown.

Make 12.

Unit 1

- Lay out the Tree blocks, the 3" red print squares, the red print setting triangles and the red print corner triangles in diagonal rows, as shown in the Assembly Diagram.

- Stitch them into rows. Join the rows.
- Finish according to *Mini Stitching Tips*, using the 1 3/4" x 44" navy blue plaid strips for the binding. ❤

Full-Size Patterns for Great-Grandmother's Scraps

(Pattern begins on page 21)

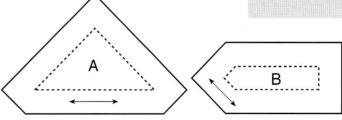

A

B

C

Full-Size Patterns for Tree of Life

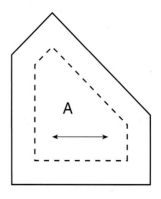

A

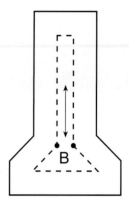

B

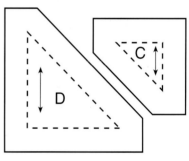

D

C

Full-Size Pattern for Indiana Stars

(Pattern begins on page 20)

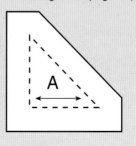

A

Wheel of Mystery

*Take the mystery out of this quilt
by experimenting with your
light and dark scraps!*

Don't be fooled—**"Wheel of Mystery"** (13 1/2" x 16") by Diane Lane of Wichita, Kansas, was appliquéd, not pieced as it may appear. The circular quilting design and the use of light and dark fabrics make this quilt seem to swirl.

QUILT SIZE: 13 1/2" x 16"
BLOCK SIZE: 2 1/2" square

MATERIALS
Yardage is estimated for 44" fabrics.
• 20 light brown scraps, each at least 4" square
• 20 dark brown scraps, each at least 4" square
• 8" x 19" strip of brown for the border
• 1/8 yard brown for the binding
• 15 1/2" x 18" piece of backing fabric
• 15 1/2" x 18" piece of batting
• Clear plastic for templates
• Permanent marker

CUTTING
Appliqué pattern piece A is full size and does not include a seam allowance. Trace around the template on the right side of the fabric and add a 1/8" to 3/16" turn-under allowance when cutting the pieces out. All other dimensions include a 1/4" seam allowance.
• Cut 10: 4" squares, light brown
• Cut 10: 4" squares, dark brown
• Cut 40: A; 4 from each of 10 dark browns
• Cut 40: A; 4 from each of 10 light browns
• Cut 2: 2" x 17" strips, brown, for the border
• Cut 2: 2" x 19" strips, brown, for the border
• Cut 2: 1 3/4" x 44" strips, brown, for the binding

PREPARATION
• Center the clear plastic over the Full-Size Block Pattern. Using a permanent marker, trace all markings onto the plastic, including the cutting lines. Cut out the template along the cutting line.
• Place the template behind a 4" brown square. Use a light source such as a light box or brightly lit window to ensure accurate placement. Using a sharp pencil, trace the appliqué design on the right side of each of the 20 squares.

DIRECTIONS
• Arrange 4 A's on a marked 4" square and pin them in place, using the pencil lines as placement guides. Appliqué them to the square, using the tip of your needle to turn the seam allowance under as you stitch around each piece. Notice that light pieces have been appliquéd to dark blocks and dark pieces have been appliquéd to light blocks. Make 20.
• Lay the appliquéd blocks face down on a clean towel and press.
• Place the plastic template over the appliquéd design aligning the design on the template with the appliquéd design. Trace around the template with a sharp pencil.
• Trim the blocks on the pencil line.
• Lay out the blocks in 5 rows of 4, alternating light and dark.
• Stitch the blocks into rows. Join the rows.
• Center and stitch the 2" x 17" brown strips to the top and bottom of the quilt and the 2" x 19" brown strips to the sides of the quilt. Start and stop stitching 1/4" from the edges and backstitch.
• Miter each corner, referring to *Mini Stitching Tips.*
• Finish according to *Mini Stitching Tips*, using the 1 3/4" x 44" brown strips for the binding. ❤

Full-Size Block Pattern for Wheel of Mystery

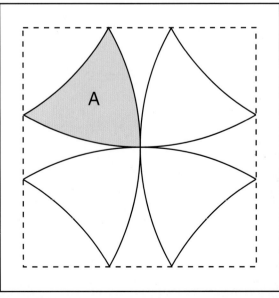

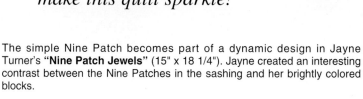

Nine Patch ❖ Jewels

Choose bright colors to make this quilt sparkle!

The simple Nine Patch becomes part of a dynamic design in Jayne Turner's **"Nine Patch Jewels"** (15" x 18 1/4"). Jayne created an interesting contrast between the Nine Patches in the sashing and her brightly colored blocks.

QUILT SIZE: 15" x 18 1/4"
BLOCK SIZE: 1 1/2" square

MATERIALS

Yardage is estimated for 44" fabric.
• 18 scraps of medium prints each at least 2" square
• 18 scraps of dark prints each at least 2" x 3"
• Scrap of medium blue print at least 9" x 12"
• 1/3 yard navy
• 1/3 yard white
• Fat eighth (11" x 18") light blue
• Fat quarter (18" x 22") navy print
• 17" x 20 1/4" piece of backing fabric
• 17" x 20 1/4" piece of thin batting

CUTTING

Dimensions include a 1/4" seam allowance.
For each of 18 blocks:
• Cut 5: 1" squares, one dark print scrap
• Cut 4: 1" squares, one medium print scrap
Also:
• Cut 10: 3/4" x 22" strips, white
• Cut 4: 3/4" x 25" strips, white
• Cut 5: 3/4" x 22" strips, navy
• Cut 5: 3/4" x 25" strips, navy
• Cut 2: 1" x 13" strips, navy, for the inner border

• Cut 2: 1" x 17" strips, navy, for the inner border
• Cut 3: 4 1/2" squares, medium blue, then cut them in quarters diagonally to yield 12 setting triangles. You will use 10.
• Cut 2: 3" squares, medium blue, then cut them in half diagonally to yield 4 corner triangles
• Cut 2: 3/4" x 14" strips, light blue, for the middle border
• Cut 2: 3/4" x 17" strips, light blue, for the middle border
• Cut 2: 1 3/4" x 14" strips, navy print, for the outer border
• Cut 2: 1 3/4" x 20" strips, navy print, for the outer border
• Cut 4: 1 3/4" x 20" strips, navy print, for the binding

DIRECTIONS

• Lay out 5 matching 1" dark print squares and 4 matching 1" medium print squares. Stitch the squares into rows. Join the rows to complete a Nine Patch block. Make 18.
• Stitch a 3/4" x 22" navy strip between two 3/4" x 22" white strips, right sides together along their length, to make a pieced strip. Press the seam allowances toward the navy strip, then trim them to 1/8". Make 5.
• From each pieced strip, cut ten 2"

slices, as shown, for the sashing strips. You will use 48.

• Stitch a 3/4" x 25" white strip between two 3/4" x 25" navy strips, right sides together along their length, to make pieced strip A. Press the seam allowances toward the navy strips, then trim them to 1/8". Make 2.
• Stitch a 3/4" x 25" navy strip between two 3/4" x 25" white strips, right sides together along their length, to make pieced strip B. Press the seam allowances toward the navy strips, then trim them to 1/8".
• From each pieced strip A, cut thirty-one 3/4" slices.
• From pieced strip B, cut thirty-one 3/4" slices.
• Lay out 3 slices, as shown. Join the slices to complete a Nine Patch sashing block. Make 31.

• Lay out the Nine Patch blocks, sashing strips, Nine Patch sashing blocks, setting triangles and corner triangles in diagonal rows. Stitch them into rows and join the rows as shown in the Assembly Diagram.
• Measure the width of the quilt. Trim

the 1" x 13" navy strips to equal that measurement. Stitch them to the short sides of the quilt.
• Measure the length of the quilt, including borders. Trim the 1" x 17" navy strips to equal that measurement. Stitch them to the long sides of the quilt.
• In the same manner, trim the 3/4" x 14" light blue strips to fit the short sides and stitch them to the quilt.
• Trim the 3/4" x 17" light blue strips to fit the long sides and stitch them to

the quilt.
• Trim the 1 3/4" x 14" navy print strips to fit the short sides and stitch them to the quilt.
• Trim the 1 3/4" x 20" navy print strips to fit the long sides and stitch them to the quilt.
• Finish according to *Mini Stitching Tips*, using the 1 3/4" x 20" navy print strips for the binding. ❤

Assembly Diagram ———→

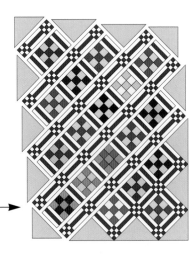

Birdhouses

This appliqué is "for the birds!"

Jean Bell of Greenville, Ohio, designed **"Birdhouses"** (12" x 12 1/2") near the end of a long, tiresome winter. Jean says she made the quilt so she could celebrate spring early inside her house!

QUILT SIZE: 12" x 12 1/2"

MATERIALS
Yardage is estimated for 44" fabric.
• Assorted scraps of brown, tan, red and blue prints for the birdhouses
• Fat eighth (11" x 18") white print, for the fence
• Fat eighth tan print, for the background
• Fat eighth beige print, for the inner border
• 1/4 yard red print for the outer border and binding
• 14" x 14 1/2" piece of backing fabric
• 14" x 14 1/2" piece of thin batting
• Embroidery floss
• Invisible nylon thread (optional)
• Black permanent marker
• Fusible web

CUTTING
Appliqué pieces are full size and do not

need a seam allowance. Trace around the pieces on the paper side of the fusible web and cut them out slightly beyond the traced line. Fuse them to the wrong side of the appropriate color scrap and cut them out on the line.
• Cut l: 8 1/2" x 9" rectangle, tan print, for the background
• Cut 4: 3/4" x 9" strips, beige print, for the inner border
• Cut 2: 2" x 9 1/2" strips, red print, for the outer border
• Cut 2: 2" x 12" strips, red print, for the outer border
• Cut 2: 1 3/4" x 44" strips, red print, for the binding

PREPARATION
• Measure in 1 1/4" from the long sides of the background rectangle and make a pencil mark. These are the placement guides for the 2 outer bird-

house posts. Make 2 more evenly spaced marks for the remaining posts.
• Measure 1/2" from the bottom of the background rectangle to mark the position of the bottom edge of the lower fence rail. Measure 2" from the bottom of the background rectangle to mark the position of the bottom edge of the upper fence rail.
• Measure in 3/8" from each side of the background rectangle and make a pencil mark. These are the placement guides for the fence posts. Make 5 more evenly spaced marks for the remaining fence posts.

DIRECTIONS
• Remove the paper from the fusible web and press the appliqué pieces to the background rectangle in the following order:
  Birdhouse posts (you need 4)

Fence rails (you need 2)
Fence posts (you need 7)
House sections of birdhouses
Roofs and bases of birdhouses

NOTE: *You may wish to secure the edges of each piece with a narrow zig-zag stitch using invisible nylon thread.*

• Stitch 3/4" x 9" beige print strips to the sides of the quilt.
• Stitch 3/4" x 9" beige print strips to the top and bottom of the quilt.
• Stitch the 2" x 9 1/2" red print strips to the sides of the quilt.
• Stitch the 2" x 12" red print strips to the top and bottom of the quilt.
• Embroider vines and flowers on the birdhouse posts using a stem stitch and lazy-daisy stitch.
• Mark the holes and perches on the birdhouses with the permanent marker.
• Finish according to *Mini Stitching Tips*, using the 1 3/4" x 44" red print strips for the binding. ❤

Full-Size Appliqué Patterns for Birdhouses

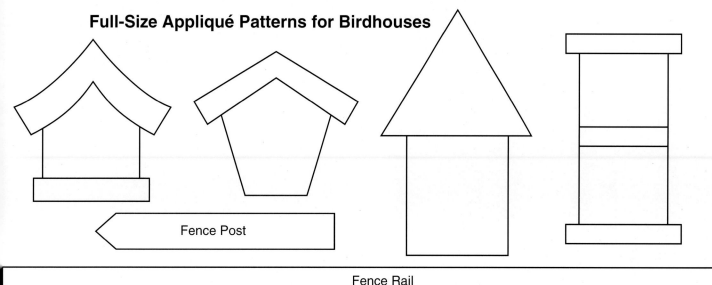

Fence Post

Fence Rail

Birdhouse Post

Gingerbread Play *(continued from page 16)*

including the borders. Trim the 1" x 16 1/2" muslin strips to equal that measurement. Stitch them to the top and bottom of the quilt.
• In the same manner, trim 2 of the 2" x 19 1/2" red plaid strips to fit the quilt's length and stitch them to the sides of the quilt.
• Trim the remaining 2" x 19 1/2" red plaid strips to fit the quilt's width and stitch them to the top and bottom of the quilt.
• Finish according to *Mini Stitching Tips*, using the 1 3/4" x 44" plaid strips for the binding.
• Stitch 1/2" buttons to the quilt, stitching through the top layer only. ❤

Assembly Diagram

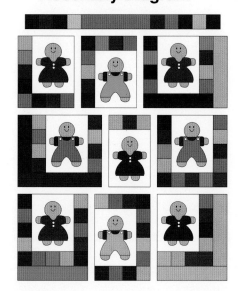

Full-Size Appliqué Patterns for Gingerbread Play

Little Houses

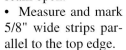

Construct your own miniature village!

Any good architect builds a house with precision and accuracy. Vivienne Moore of Martinez, California, did the same by constructing **"Little Houses"** (16 1/2" x 20 1/4") with foundation piecing.

QUILT SIZE: 16 1/2" x 20 1/4"
BLOCK SIZE: 3" square

MATERIALS
Yardage is estimated for 44" fabric.
• Dark, medium and light scraps for the houses
• 1/8 yard red
• 1/2 yard navy
• Medium green scraps for leaves
• 12" square of green for the vine
• 18 1/2" x 22 1/2" piece of backing fabric
• 18 1/2" x 22 1/2" piece of batting
• Permanent marker
• Paper, muslin or lightweight, non-fusible interfacing for the foundations
• 3 yards of yarn
• Marking chalk

CUTTING
Dimensions include a 1/4" seam allowance. Fabric for foundation piecing will be cut as you sew the blocks. Each piece should be at least 1/2" larger on all sides than the section it will cover. Refer to Mini Stitching Tips *as needed.*
• Cut 2: 1 3/4" x 44" strips, navy, for the binding

• Cut 2: 2 1/4" x 22" strips, navy, for the outer border
• Cut 4: 3/4" x 22" strips, navy
• Cut 2: 2 1/4" x 14" strips, navy, for the outer border
• Cut 31: 1 1/4" x 3 1/2" strips, navy, for the sashing
• Cut 5: 3/4" x 22" strips, red
• Cut 2: 3/4" x 18" strips, red, for the inner border
• Cut 2: 3/4" x 14" strips, red, for the inner border
• Cut 36: Leaves, various shades of green
NOTE: *The appliqué leaf pattern is full size and does not include a seam allowance. Trace around the template on the right side of the fabric and add 1/8" to 3/16" turn-under allowance when cutting the pieces out.*

PREPARATION
• To make a continuous green bias strip 5/8" wide, cut the 12" green square in half diagonally. Make a diamond from the cut square, as shown. Stitch the 2 triangles together and press the seam open.
• Measure and mark 5/8" wide strips parallel to the top edge.
• With right sides together and edges offset as shown, stitch the edges together to form a cylinder.

• Cut along the marked lines starting at the top of the cylinder and continuing to the bottom. You will need approximately 100".

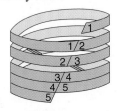

DIRECTIONS
Follow the foundation piecing instructions in Mini Stitching Tips *to piece the blocks.*

- Trace the 4 full-size patterns 12 times each on the foundation material, transferring all lines and numbers and leaving a 1" space between foundations. Cut each one out 1/2" beyond the broken line.

For the Chimney section:
- Use the following fabrics in these positions:
  - 1 - sky fabric
  - 2, 3 - chimney fabric
  - 4, 5 - sky fabric

For the Roof section:
- Use the following fabrics in these positions:
  - 1 - chimney fabric
  - 2 - first house fabric
  - 3, 4 - sky fabric

For the Window section:
- Use the following fabrics in these positions:
  - 1 - second house fabric
  - 2, 3 - window fabric
  - 4, 5, 6, 7 - second house fabric

For the Door section:
- Use the following fabrics in these positions:
  - 1 - door fabric
  - 2, 3, 4 - first house fabric
- Baste each foundation in the seam allowance, halfway between the stitching line and the broken line, to hold the fabrics in place.
- Trim each foundation on the broken line.
- Stitch a Chimney section to a Roof section, as shown, to make the top half of a House block.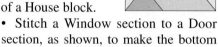
- Stitch a Window section to a Door section, as shown, to make the bottom half of a House block.

- Join the top half and the bottom half to make a House block. Make 12.

For the Nine Patch blocks:
- Stitch a 3/4" x 22" navy strip between two 3/4" x 22" red strips to make a pieced strip. Trim the seams to 1/8". Make 2.
- Cut forty 3/4" slices from the pieced

strips. Label them A.
- Stitch a 3/4" x 22" red strip between two 3/4" x 22" navy strips to make a pieced strip. Trim the seams to 1/8".
- Cut twenty 3/4" slices from the pieced strip. Label them B.
- Lay out 2 A slices and a B slice. Join them to make a Nine Patch, as shown. Make 20.
- Referring to the photo, lay out the House blocks, the 1 1/4" x 3 1/2" navy sashing strips and the Nine Patches.
- Stitch the Nine Patches and sashing strips into rows. Stitch the houses and sashing strips into rows. Join the rows.
- Measure the width of the quilt. Trim the 3/4" x 14" red strips to equal that measurement. Stitch them to the top and bottom of the quilt.
- Measure the length of the quilt, including the borders. Trim the 3/4" x 18" red strips to equal that measurement. Stitch them to the sides of the quilt.
- In the same manner, trim the 2 1/4" x 14" navy strips to fit the quilt's width and stitch them to the top and bottom

of the quilt.
- Trim the 2 1/4" x 22" navy strips to fit the remaining sides and stitch them to the quilt.
- If you used paper foundations, remove them now.
- Lay the green bias strip wrong side up, on an ironing board. Fold 1/3 of the strip, wrong side in, as shown. Press.

- Referring to the photo, use the yarn as a guide for vine placement, laying the yarn in undulating curves along the border. Pin the yarn in place, then trace its outline with chalk. Remove the pins and yarn.
- Pin the green bias strip on the traced line, 2" to 3" at a time, with the folded edge toward the inside of the quilt. Appliqué the folded edge, then use the tip of your needle to fold the raw edge under as you appliqué the vine in place.
- Referring to the photo, appliqué the leaves to the quilt.
- Finish according to *Mini Stitching Tips*, using the 1 3/4" x 44" navy strips for the binding. ❤

Full-Size Foundation Patterns for Little Houses

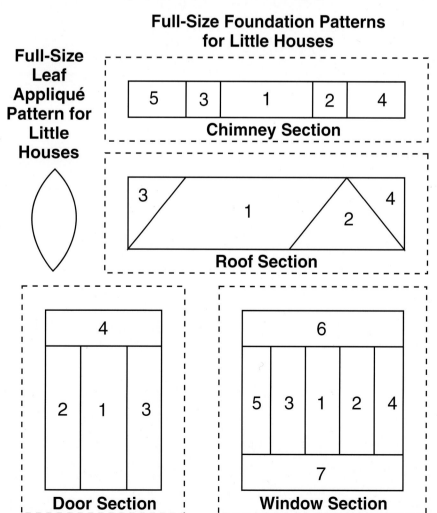

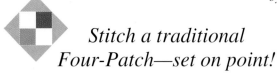

More Than Just a Four Patch

by Lynne M. Trace

Stitch a traditional Four-Patch—set on point!

"More Than Just a Four Patch" (14" x 17"), was made by Lynne M. Trace of Elliottsburg, Pennsylvania. Lynne found inspiration for this mini scrappy quilt on the cover of *Traditonal Quiltworks* magazine Issue #12, which featured Sharyn Craig's "4-Patch Delight."

QUILT SIZE: 14" x 17"
BLOCK SIZE: 2 7/8" square

MATERIALS

Yardage is estimated for 44" fabric.
- 8 dark print strips each at least 1 1/2" x 15"
- 8 light print strips each at least 1 1/2" x 15"
- 1/4 yard green print for 6 blocks and the binding
- Piece of pink print at least 7 1/2" x 10"
- 1" x 44" strip of brown print for the inner border
- 16" x 19" piece of backing fabric
- 16" x 19" piece of thin batting

CUTTING

All dimensions include a 1/4" seam allowance.
- Cut 8: 1 1/2" x 15" strips, assorted dark prints
- Cut 8: 1 1/2" x 15" strips, assorted light prints
- Cut 12: 2 1/2" squares, green print, then cut them in half diagonally to yield 24 triangles
- Cut 12: 2 1/2" squares, pink print, then cut them in half diagonally to yield 24 triangles
- Cut 2: 1 3/4" x 44" strips, green print, for the binding

DIRECTIONS

- Stitch a 1 1/2" x 15" light print strip to a 1 1/2" x 15" dark print strip, right sides together along their length. Press the seam allowance toward the dark fabric. Make 8.
- Cut four 1 1/2" segments and three 2 1/2" segments from each pieced strip.

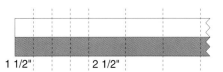

- Join two 1 1/2" segments, as shown to make a Four Patch block. Make 16.

- Stitch 2 pink print triangles to opposite sides of a Four Patch. Press the seam allowance toward the triangles. Stitch 2 pink print triangles to the remaining sides of the Four Patch to make a block. Press the seam allowance toward the triangles. Make 6.

- In the same manner, make 6 blocks using the green print triangles.
- Trim the pieced blocks to 3 3/8".
- Referring to the photo, lay out the pieced blocks in 4 rows of 3. Stitch the blocks into rows. Join the rows.
- Measure the width of the quilt. Cut 2 lengths from the 1" x 44" inner border strip each equal to that measurement. Stitch them to the short sides of the quilt.
- Measure the length of the quilt, including the borders. Cut 2 lengths from the inner border strip each equal to that measurement. Stitch them to the long sides of the quilt.
- Join five 2 1/2" segments to make a short pieced border. Make 2.
- Measure the width of the quilt. Trim the short pieced borders to equal that measurement.
- Stitch a Four Patch to each end of the short pieced borders. Set them aside.
- Join seven 2 1/2" pieced segments to make a long pieced border. Make 2.
- Stitch the long pieced borders to the long sides of the quilt. Trim the excess from the borders.
- Stitch the short pieced borders to the remaining sides of the quilt.
- Finish according to *Mini Stitching Tips*, using the 1 3/4" x 44" green print strips for the binding. ❤

Mini Stitching Tips

Fabric Selection

We recommend 100% cotton for most projects because it is easy to finger press and handles nicely. The yardage requirements in our patterns are based on a standard 44" wide bolt. However, many of the quilts can be made from assorted scraps.

Fabric Preparation

We suggest washing your fabrics before using them in your minis. Test all of your fabrics to be sure they are colorfast.

Templates

Trace pattern pieces on clear plastic. Use a permanent marker to list the name of the block, total number of pieces, pattern letter and grainline on each template. If the instructions call for an R, for example BR, the B template must be reversed before tracing.

Pieced Patterns

Unless otherwise noted, our patterns include 1/4" seam allowances. The solid line is the cutting line and the broken line is the sewing line. For machine piecing, make the template with the seam allowance. Trace around the template on the right side of the fabric. For hand piecing, make the template without the seam allowance. Trace the template on the wrong side of the fabric flipping all directional (asymetrical) templates before tracing and add 1/4" seam allowance as you cut.

Foundation Pieced Patterns

Foundation piecing is a method for making even the smallest blocks with a high degree of accuracy. For each foundation, trace all of the lines and numbers onto paper, muslin or lightweight non-fusible interfacing. You will need one foundation for each block or part of a block. The solid line is the stitching line and the broken line is the cutting line. The fabric pieces you select do not have to be cut precisely. Be generous when cutting fabric pieces as excess fabric will be trimmed away after sewing. Your goal is to cut a piece that covers the numbered area and extends into surrounding areas

after seams are stitched. Generally, fabric pieces should be large enough to extend 1/2" beyond the seamline on all sides before stitching. For very small sections, or sections without angles, 1/4" may be sufficient. Select a short stitch length, 12-14 stitches per inch.

Place fabric pieces on the unmarked side of the foundation and stitch on the marked side. Center the first piece, right side up, over section 1 on the unmarked side of the foundation. Hold the foundation up to a light to make sure that the raw edges of the fabric extend at least 1/2" beyond the seamline on all sides. Hold this first piece in place with a small dab of glue or a pin. Place the fabric for section 2 on the first piece, right sides together. Turn the foundation over and sew on the line between 1 and 2, extending the stitching past the beginning and end of the line by a few stitches on both ends. Trim the seam allowance to 1/8". Fold the section 2 piece back, right side up, and press. Continue adding pieces to the foundation in the same manner until all sections are covered and the block is complete.

If you are using a muslin or interfacing foundation, it will become a permanent part of the quilt. If you are using paper, it will be removed. However, do not remove the paper until the blocks have been joined together and at least one border has been added, to avoid disturbing the stitches. Use tweezers to carefully remove sections of the paper. The pieces will be perforated from the stitching and can be gently pulled free.

Appliqué Patterns

A seam allowance is not included on appliqué pieces. The solid line is the sewing line. Make a template and lightly trace around it on the right side of the fabric. Then "eyeball" a 1/8" to 3/16" turn-under allowance when cutting the fabric. Clip inside curves almost to the pencil line so they will turn under smoothly as you stitch.

Marking Fabric

We suggest using silver or white

marking tools for dark fabrics and fine line pencils for light fabrics. Always use a sharp pencil and a light touch. Lay a piece of fine-grained sandpaper under the fabric to keep it from slipping while you mark it.

Hand Sewing

Use a thin, short needle ("sharp") to ensure a flat seam. Sew only on the marked sewing line using small, even stitches.

Needleturn Appliqué

Pin an appliqué piece in position on the background fabric. Using thread to match the appliqué piece, thread a needle with a 15" to 18" length and knot one end. Turn under the allowance and bring the needle from the wrong side of the background fabric up through the fold on the marked line of the appliqué piece. Push the needle through the background fabric, catching a few threads, and come back up through the appliqué piece on the marked line close to the first stitch. Use the point of the needle to smooth under the allowance and make another stitch in the same way. Continue needle-turning and stitching until the piece is completely sewn to the background fabric. To reduce bulk, do not stitch where one appliqué piece will be overlapped by another.

Machine Sewing

Set the stitch length to 14 stitches per inch. Cut a length of masking tape or moleskin foot pad about 1/4" x 2". Place a clear plastic ruler under and to the left of the needle aligning the right edge of the ruler 1/4" from the point of the needle along the throat plate. Stick the masking tape or moleskin in place at the ruler's edge. Feed fabric under the needle, touching this guide.

When directions call for you to start or stop stitching 1/4" from edges, as for set-in pieces, backstitch to secure the seam.

Pressing

Press seams toward the darker of the two fabrics. Press abutting seams in opposite directions whenever possible. Use a dry iron and press carefully, as little blocks are easy to distort.

Making Bias Strips

Most miniature work requires bias strips of 25" or less. Begin with an 18" fabric square. Lay your clear plastic ruler diagonally across the square and cut from corner to corner. Cut a bias strip the width you require, measuring from the diagonal cut. This strip will be 25". Additional diagonal cuts will decrease in length. Cut as many as required for your pattern.

Mitering Corners

For mitered borders, the pattern allows extra length on each border strip. Stitch each border to the quilt top, beginning, ending and backstitching each seamline 1/4" from the edge of the quilt top. After all borders have been attached in this manner, miter one corner at a time. With the quilt top lying right side down, lay one border over the other. Draw a straight line at a 45° angle from the inner corner to the outer corner, as shown.

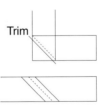

Reverse the positions of the borders and mark another straight line from corner to corner, in the same manner.

Place the borders, right sides together, with marked seamlines carefully matched and pinned and stitch from the outer to the inner corner backstitching at the inner corner. Open the mitered seam to make sure it lies flat, trim excess fabric and press.

FINISHING

Marking

Cut simple designs from clear plastic adhesive-backed shelf paper. They'll stick and re-stick long enough to finish the quilt. Use masking tape to mark grids. Remove the tape when you're not quilting to avoid leaving a sticky residue. Mark lightly with pencils; thick lines that won't go away really stand out on a small quilt.

Batting

Use a low-loft or very thin batting. Some quilters peel batting into two layers (leaving some loft and good drape);

others use flannel as a filler. Layer the quilt sandwich as follows: backing, wrong side up; batting; quilt top, right side up. Baste or pin the layers together.

Quilting

Very small quilts can be lap-quilted without a hoop. Larger ones can be quilted in a hoop or small frame. Use a short, thin needle ("between") and small stitches that will be in scale with the little quilt. Thread the needle with a single strand of quilting thread and knot one end. Insert the needle through the quilt top and batting (not the backing) an inch away from where you want to begin quilting. Gently pull the thread to pop the knot through the top and bury it in the batting. Our experience is that too much quilting can flatten a miniature and set the quilt "out of square." Too little quilting causes puffiness which can detract from the scale of the quilt. Experiment and decide what you like best. When the quilting is finished, trim the back and batting even with the top.

Binding

For most straight-edged quilts, a double-fold French binding is an attractive, durable and easy finish. NOTE: *If your quilt has curved or scalloped edges, binding strips must be cut on the bias of the fabric.* To make 1/4" finished binding, cut each strip 1 3/4" wide. Sew binding strips (cross-grain or bias) together with diagonal seams; trim and press seams open.

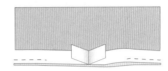

Fold the binding strip in half lengthwise, wrong sides together and press. Position the binding strip on the right side of the quilt top, aligning the raw edges of the binding with the edge of the quilt top. Leave approximately 4" of the binding strip free. Beginning several inches from one corner, stitch the binding to the quilt with a 1/4" seam allowance. When you reach a corner, stop the stitching line exactly 1/4" from the edge. Backstitch, clip threads and remove the quilt from the machine. Fold the binding up and away, creating a 45° angle, as shown.

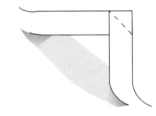

Fold the binding down as shown, and begin stitching at the edge.

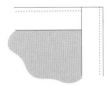

Continue stitching around the quilt to within 4" of the starting point. To finish, fold both strips back along the edge of the quilt so that the folded edges meet an equal distance from both lines of stitching and the binding lies flat on the quilt. Finger press to crease the folds. Cut both strips 7/8" from the folds.

Open both strips and place the ends at right angles to each other, right sides together. Fold the bulk of the quilt out of your way. Join the strips with a diagonal seam, as shown.

Trim the seam to 1/4" and press it open. Fold the joined strips so that the wrong sides are together again. Place the binding flat against the quilt and finish stitching it to the quilt. Clip the corners. Trim the batting and backing even with the edge of the quilt top so that the binding edge will be filled with batting when you fold the binding to the back of the quilt. Blindstitch the binding to the back of the quilt, covering the seamline.

Sign Your Quilt

Small quilts are revered by collectors, and the little quilts we make today will be treasured by our families and friends. Using embroidery, cross-stitch or permanent marker, write your name and other important data like your city, the date the quilt was completed and for whom the quilt was made somewhere on the back, or attach a label. Someone will be glad you did!